Vocabulary to Teach Kids

30 days to increased vocabulary and improved reading comprehension

Julie Jones

© www.beststudentsuccesssseries.com

ISBN:
ISBN-13: 978-0-9842493-1-2
ISBN-10: 0-9842493-1-1
eISBN-13: 978-0-9842493-2-9
eISBN-10: 0-9842493-2-X

Library of Congress Control Number: 2015915672

© www.beststudentsuccessseries.com

DEDICATION

I love you, Victor, my son. You will never know how much I love you and appreciate your help.

PAGE LEFT BLANK INTENTIONALLY

CONTENTS

1   Parent Letter   1

2   Student Letter   5

3   Lesson 1   7

4   Lesson 2   16

5   Lesson 3   25

6   Answers   35

7   Bibliography   45

PAGE LEFT BLANK INTENTIONALLY

PARENT LETTER

Dear Parent,

Are you tired of your school system failing to provide an adequate education for your child? I was too which is why I wrote this book especially once I realized that the common core curriculum isn't the change students need. The common core curriculum only tells schools what need to be taught by grade level and not how to teach it. As a parent like me, you know there are good teachers as well as bad so what does that mean to the curriculum? Everything is status quo. What does it mean for your child? The standards are going to get tougher so you must do what you can to help your child. This is where this book comes in. This book is researched based and designed to increase your child's vocabulary and improve his or her's reading comprehension within in 30 days.

How? This book teaches the most common prefixes using everyday words so that it is easy for your child to remember and grasp. This is important because it will make it easier for your child to understand words he is not familiar with while reading books, doing school work and understand information on standardized test better.

The book contains 3 lessons which provide 5 activities for each lesson. It is assumed that your child can read, knows how to use a dictionary and thesaurus, knows what a synonym and antonym is, can write in complete sentences and knows how to complete a crossword puzzle. Each lesson builds on to the next by showing your child how to understand words.

To give your child the most benefit to the lessons completed in this book, it is important that you stick to a strict schedule so that your child completes it the lessons in 30 days. How will you do this? I understand that life happens such as homework, extracurricular activities, etc. So, in order to help you stay on track with the 30 days schedule, I make the following suggestions:

- Use calendar to identify your start month and year
- Use a calendar to mark the days and time you plan to complete the lessons (see page 4)
- Use a timer so that you can keep the time used to a minimum and fit everything in (your cell phone has a timer so you don't have to buy one)
- Make an agreement with your child regarding completing the lessons so that they know what is expected of them when and at what time

These are actions I had to incorporate into my routine to make sure that my child completed the lessons in 30 days, completed his other homework, enjoyed other activities and got into bed on time. How? I had my son complete one activity per day using a five day week meaning Monday through Friday with weekends off. Just like his school schedule. However, if he had a test or more than average homework, I would either time him on his regular school work so he could fit in the extra activity or have him do it on the weekend. I am sharing this with you so that you can get an idea on how to fit everything into the 30 days too.

In addition to the calendar, I have included a template (example) of a contract (see page 3) for you to set up an agreement between you and your child. Why? I know that kids fuss and fight sometimes regarding getting things done. By establishing a contract between you and your child, you will be able to keep the focus on getting the activities or worksheets done. I also recommend that you have your child write the entire contract out while inputting your names in the blanks. Then, have him or her reread what they wrote before both of you sign it. Simply make sure you make any changes you want to the contract before you dictate it to him/ her. Please keep the signed contract in a safe place just in case you need it later.

If you stick with the program and complete it within 30 days, you will see a big improvement in your child's vocabulary and reading comprehension. If you have any questions, you can email me at Julie@beststudentsuccessseries.com. Thank you for your purchase of this book.

Best regards,

Here is a sample contract for you to use with your child. I recommend that you have your child copy the contract on a separate piece of paper along with any additions you want to make which is specific to your situation.

Contract

I, name of your child, promise to complete the activities in the workbook on days you agree to complete it on at the time you agree upon. If something happens such as I, student's name, have too much home work on the scheduled day. I will complete the assignment on the next day at the scheduled time without fussing, fighting or arguing.

Signed,

Your child's name and parent's / guardian's name

Please use the following calendar to schedule when you are going to complete the assignments. I am making this suggestion because I found it very helpful to make a schedule complete with the dates and times the assignment was going to be complete. Why? Because I could remember to fit it into our routine and was able to remind my son what was expected of him.

[Month] [Year] Calendar

Sunday ▼	Monday ▼	Tuesday ▼	Wednesday ▼	Thursday ▼	Friday ▼	Saturday ▼

STUDENT LETTER

Hi! My name is Julie and I wrote this book. I hope that you find this book helpful. Do you want a way to improve your grades with minimal (little) effort? If so, read on...

Why I wrote this book? I wrote this book because no matter how technology changes you will always need to read something such as a computer, electronic pad, etc. to learn information. This means being able to read is a vital (very important) skill to have. In order to develop (expand) this skill, you must understand words because it leads to increased vocabulary and improved reading comprehension.

How will you learn to understand words? Words are made up of prefix, suffixes and root words. In this book, each of the 3 lessons teach you the meaning of the most common prefixes. Each of these 3 lessons has 5 activities each. Here is a list of the activities you will complete during each lesson along with what you will learn:

1) Activity 1 is a word study or word analysis exercise. You will look up the meaning of the word in a dictionary such as dictionary.com, ldceonline.com or oxforddictionaries.com. You can even use an old fashioned book, but the point I want to emphasize it that you must use a reputable (reliable) dictionary with standard language. Tip: When looking up the word, make sure to read all of the definitions because so words have multiple (many) meanings. Also, read the sentences to see how the words are used in sentences. This will help you when you do Activity 2.

   During the word analysis, you will also need to write a synonym (similar) or antonym (opposite) word meaning. This will help you understand the word better.

2) Activity 2 is a fill in the blank exercise. You will use the words which you looked up in Activity 1 to fill in the blank. How? By using context (hints from the surrounding words) clues to figure out which word to put in the blank

3) Activity 3 is to look for patterns in the definition of words with the same prefix. Each word has a similar meaning because of the prefix. For example, the prefix re- means again or back. The words repair and restore begin with the prefix re-. The word repair means to restore to sound condition after damage or injury. The word restore means to bring back to an original condition. (See figure 1).

Word	Definition
repair	to restore to sound condition after damage or injury
restore	to bring back to an original condition

Figure 1. The words repair and restore have similar meanings because each word has something to do with returning something back to an original condition.

4) Activity 4 is another word analysis or study activity. The difference is that you will complete the assignment using words you know that begin with the prefix from the lesson. Then, you will need to do a word study of those words.

5) Activity 5 is a crossword puzzle.

All of these activities together will increase your vocabulary and improve your reading comprehension. How? You will be able to use context clues and breakdown the prefixes of words so that you can figure out the meaning words you may not be familiar with. Good luck!

LESSON 1

As discussed in the student letter, you will learn the meaning of the following prefixes through 5 activities:

Word Bank of Prefixes		
	Anti – against	Ex- out of; from
Under- below, less than	Dis- not; opposite	Non- not

As you complete each activity, I want you think about how you can use the knowledge of knowing prefixes to improve your reading comprehension, your writing and your communication skills.

I recommend that you use http://www.dictionary.com, oxforddictionaries.com and an actual dictionary to complete the activities. Let's get started!..

Lesson 1: Prefixes: anti-, dis-, ex-, non-, under-

Word Bank of Prefixes		
	Anti – against	Ex- out of; from
Under- below, less than	Dis- not; opposite	Non- not

Word Study or Analysis: Do a word study or analysis of the above prefixes by using of the words below, each word contains one of the prefixes. REMEMBER to look for patterns in the definitions of words with the same prefix.

Word	Definition	Synonym	Antonym
antivirus			
antisocial			
antidote			
antifreeze			
antibody			
ex-student			
ex-president			
ex-member			
explain			
exist			
disappear			
disagree			
dislike			
disconnect			
disgrace			
nonsense			
nonstop			
nonviolent			
nonfiction			
underweight			
understudy			
underwater			
underground			

Lesson 1: Prefixes: anti-, dis-, ex-, non-, under-

On the previous page, did you notice how the words with the same suffixes have similar meaning?

Word Bank of Prefixes		
	Anti - against	Ex- out of; from
Under- below, less than	Dis- not; opposite	Non- not

Fill in the blank.

1. The train travels _____ground.
2. The _____virus software was installed to protect the computer.
3. He is a great _____fiction writer.
4. I _____like going to that store,
5. She is an _____member of the team.
6. He is acting very _____social by watching too much TV.
7. He is the _____president of the student council.
8. She is the _____study of the leader character in the play.
9. He tried to _____agree with the debate team.
10. All the talk about the storm turned out to be _____sense.
11. Each _____body has a different type of germ.
12. He walked off in _____grace.
13. There was a _____connect when he explained the solution to the problem.
14. Many people believe Big Foot does _____ist.
15. The protestors lead a _____violent demonstration.
16. The airline had to _____plain the time delay.
17. The baby was born _____weight.
18. He watched the car _____appear down the road,
19. She is an _____student of that school.
20. The train traveled _____stop from New York to Washington DC.
21. The car ran out of _____freeze.
22. After the snake bite, the hiker had to wait for the _____dote.
23. The resort had an _____water aquarium.

Lesson 1: Prefixes: anti-, dis-, ex-, non-, under-

Word Bank of Prefixes		
	Anti-	Ex-
Under-	Dis-	Non-

Question: What pattern do I see in the meaning of the words with the same prefix? Answer in complete sentences.

1. What is the pattern I see in the meaning of words that begin with the prefix anti-?

_____

_____

2. What is the pattern I see in the meaning of words that begin with the prefix dis-?

_____

_____

3. What is the pattern I see in the meaning of words that begin with the prefix ex-?

_____

_____

4. What is the pattern I see in the meaning of words that begin with the prefix non-?

_____

_____

5. What is the pattern I see in the meaning of words that begin with the prefix under-?

_____

_____

Lesson 1: Prefixes: anti-, dis-, ex-, non-, under-

Now, it's your turn. **Do-It Yourself** (DIY) word study. Think of words you know which begin with the prefixes learned in this lesson. Do a word study on the words you think of.

1. Do you know any words that begin with anti-? List 2. (If you don't know any, look in the dictionary.)

_____

2. Do a word study on your 2 words.

Word	Definition	Synonym	Antonym

3. Do you know any words that begin with dis-? List 2. (If you don't know any, look in the dictionary.)

_____

4. Do a word study on your 2 words.

Word	Definition	Synonym	Antonym

5. Do you know any words that begin with ex-? List 2. (If you don't know any, look in the dictionary.)

_____

6. Do a word study on your 2 words.

Word	Definition	Synonym	Antonym

Lesson 1: Prefixes: anti-, dis-, ex-, non-, under-

Now, it's your turn. **Do-It Yourself** (DIY) word study. Think of words you know which begin with the prefixes learned in this lesson. Do a word study on the words you think of. (continued from previous page)

7. Do you know any words that begin with non-? List 2. (If you don't know any, look in the dictionary.)

_____

8. Do a word study on your 2 words.

Word	Definition	Synonym	Antonym

Lesson 1: Prefixes: anti-, dis-, ex-, non-, under-

Crossword Puzzle Lesson 1

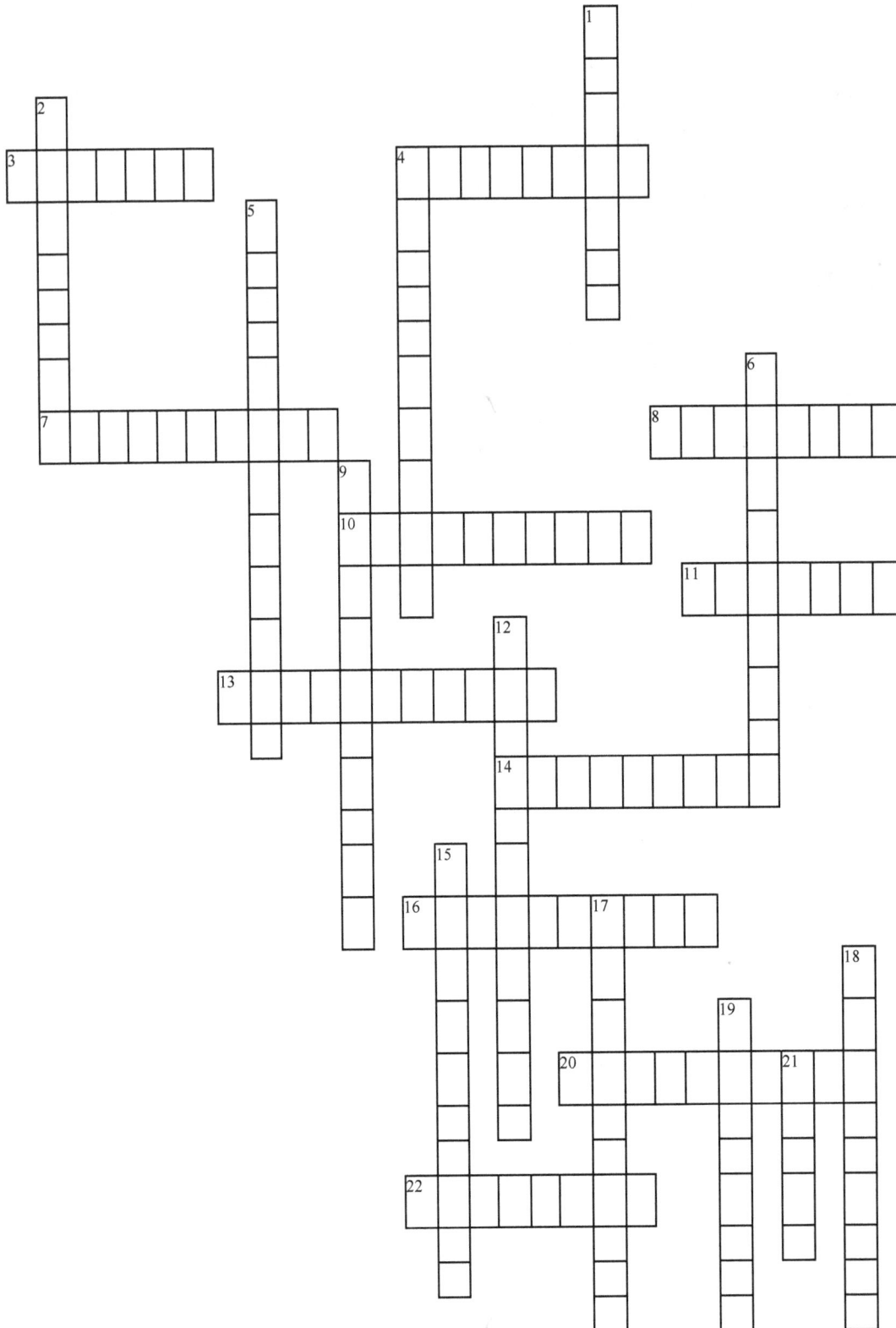

Lesson 1: Prefixes: anti-, dis-, ex-, non-, under-

Across

3. to have hatred toward something

4. craziness, ridiculousness

7. former student

8. a medicine or other remedy for counteracting the effects of poison, disease, etc.

10. story based on real facts and information

11. to make plain or clear

13. beneath the surface of the ground

14. former member

16. underneath the water's surface

20. to take apart

22. to argue

Down

1. continuous, direct

2. the loss of respect, honor, or esteem

4. peaceful

5. former president

6. to cease to be visible

9. substitute for another actor

12. deficiency in weight below a standard or requirement

15. avoiding the company of other people

17. a liquid used in the radiator of an internal-combustion engine to lower the freezing point of the cooling medium

18. a piece of software designed to prevent viruses entering a computer system or network

19. any of numerous Y -shaped protein molecules produced by B cells as a primary immune defense, each molecule and its clones having a unique binding site that can combine with the complementary site of a foreign antigen, as on a virus or bacterium, thereby disabling the antigen and signaling other immune defenses

21. to be living

Word Bank

antivirus	ex-student	disappear	nonsense	underweight
antisocial	ex-president	disagree	nonstop	understudy
antidote	ex-member	dislike	nonviolent	underwater
antifreeze	explain	disconnect	nonfiction	underground
antibody	exist	disgrace		

Review Lesson 1: Prefixes: anti-, dis-, ex-, non-, under-

Now that you have finished lesson 1 which helped you understand the meaning of the following prefixes:

Anti-

Dis-

Ex-

Non-

Under-

You should see your reading comprehension, writing and communications skills improve.

Answer the following questions: (There are no right or wrong answers.)

1) Did you find this lesson helpful? Why or why not?

_____

_____

2) What 3 things are you going to do differently as a result of this lesson when you read a book or text or have an assignment?

_____

_____

3) Do you think knowing these prefixes will improve your communication skills?

_____

4) Do you think knowing these prefixes will improve your reading comprehension?

_____

_____

LESSON 2

As discussed in the student letter, you will learn the meaning of the following prefixes through 5 activities:

Word Bank of Prefixes		
de- remove from; opposite	en-, em- cause to	in- not
re- again	un- not	

As you complete each activity, I want you think about how you can use the knowledge of knowing prefixes to improve your reading comprehension, your writing and your communication skills.

I recommend that you use http://www.dictionary.com, oxforddictionaries.com and an actual dictionary to complete the activities. Let's get started!..

Lesson 2: Prefixes: de-, em-, en-, in-, re-, un-

Word Bank of Prefixes		
de- remove from; opposite	en-, em- cause to	in- not
re- again	un- not	

Word Study or Analysis: Do a word study or analysis of the above prefixes by using of the words below, each word contains one of the prefixes. REMEMBER to look for patterns in the definitions of words with the same prefix.

	Word	Definition	Synonym	Antonym
1.	decide			
2.	depend			
3.	destroy			
4.	determine			
5.	develop			
6.	envelope			
7.	encounter			
8.	enjoy			
9.	emotional			
10.	embarrass			
11.	incomplete			
12.	incapable			
13.	independent			
14.	investigate			
15.	interpret			
16.	repair			
17.	restore			
18.	repaint			
19.	remember			
20.	unable			
21.	unbelievable			
22.	unconditional			
23.	unseen			

Lesson 2: Prefixes: de-, em-, en-, in-, re-, un-

Word Bank of Prefixes		
de- remove from; opposite	en-, em- cause to	in- not
re- again; back	un- not	

Word Bank				
decide	envelope	incomplete	repair	unable
depend	encounter	incapable	restore	unbelievable
destroy	enjoy	independent	repaint	unconditional
determine	emotional	investigate	remember	unseen
develop	embarrass	interpret		

Fill in the blank.

1. He needs to _____ whether or not to go to the party.

2. I can _____ on my mom to pick me up from school.

3. The contractor had to _____ the house before rebuilding it.

4. The science lab report was written to _____ the results of the experiment.

5. The teacher told me I had to _____ my story further because it wasn't long enough.

6. He needs an _____ to send his grandmother a letter by snail mail.

7. He had an _____ with his nemesis.

8. I really _____ the holidays because I get to see family and friends as well as eat good food.

9. He gets very _____ when it's time to take a test and he didn't study.

10. My mom likes to _____ me by telling my friends stories about me as a baby.

11. The teacher marked my homework _____ because I didn't finish it.

12. When he sings, he sings it sounds like someone is scratching a chalkboard so you know he is _____ of carrying a tune.

13. In science lab, I acted as an _____ observer for another group.

14. We used a microscope to _____ the skin of an onion.

Lesson 2: Prefixes: de-, em-, en-, in-, re-, un-

<table>
<tr><td colspan="3" align="center">Word Bank of Prefixes</td></tr>
<tr><td>de- remove from; opposite</td><td>en-, em- cause to</td><td>in- not</td></tr>
<tr><td>re- again</td><td>un- not</td><td></td></tr>
</table>

		Word Bank		
decide	envelope	incomplete	repair	unable
depend	encounter	incapable	restore	unbelievable
destroy	enjoy	independent	repaint	unconditional
determine	emotional	investigate	remember	unseen
develop	embarrass	interpret		

(continued from previous page)

15. Mom had to measure the size of the window to _____ the size of blinds to buy.

16. After the car broke down, the owner had to find a _____ shop.

17. When the computer froze, I had to perform a system _____ by turning the computer off and on.

18. He had to _____ the house when the old paint started peeling.

19. I have to _____ the date of my math test.

20. He was sad because he was _____ to go on the field trip.

21. The way he told the story made it _____ because I never heard of anything like that happening before.

22. His loyalty to his family is _____.

23. The movie had an _____ narrator.

Lesson 2: Prefixes: de-, em-, en-, in-, re-, un-

Word Bank of Prefixes		
de- remove from; opposite	en-, em- cause to	in- not
re- again	un- not	

Question: What pattern do I see in the meaning of the words with the same prefix? Answer in complete sentences

1. What is the pattern I see in the meaning of the words that begin with the prefix de-?

_____

_____

2. What is the pattern I see in the meaning of the words that begin with the prefix em- and en-?

_____

_____

3. What is the pattern I see in the meaning of the words that begin with the prefix in-?

_____

_____

4. What is the pattern I see in the meaning of the words that begin with the prefix re-?

_____

_____

5. What is the pattern I see in the meaning of the words that begin with the prefix un-?

_____

_____

Lesson 2: Prefixes: de-, em-, en-, in-, re-, un-

Now, it's your turn. **Do-It Yourself** (DIY) word study. Think of words you know which begin with the prefixes learned in this lesson. Do a word study on the words you think of.

1. Do you know any words that begin with de-? List 2. (If you don't know any, look in the dictionary.)

_____

2. Do a word study on your 2 words.

Word	Definition	Synonym	Antonym

3. Do you know any words that begin with em- and en-? List 2. (If you don't know any, look in the dictionary.)

_____

4. Do a word study on your 2 words.

Word	Definition	Synonym	Antonym

5. Do you know any words that begin with in-? List 2. (If you don't know any, look in the dictionary.)

_____

6. Do a word study on your 2 words.

Word	Definition	Synonym	Antonym

Lesson 2:   Prefixes: de-, em-, en-, in-, re-, un-

Now, it's your turn. **Do-It Yourself** (DIY) word study. Think of words you know which begin with the prefixes learned in this lesson. Do a word study on the words you think of. (continued from previous page)

7. Do you know any words that begin with re-? List 2. (If you don't know any, look in the dictionary.)

_____

8. Do a word study on your 2 words.

Word	Definition	Synonym	Antonym

9. Do you know any words that begin with un-? List 2. (If you don't know any, look in the dictionary.)

_____

10. Do a word study on your 2 words.

Word	Definition	Synonym	Antonym

PAGE LEFT INTENTIONALLY BLANK

Lesson 2: Prefixes: de-, en-, em-, in-, re-, un-

Crossword Puzzle Lesson 2

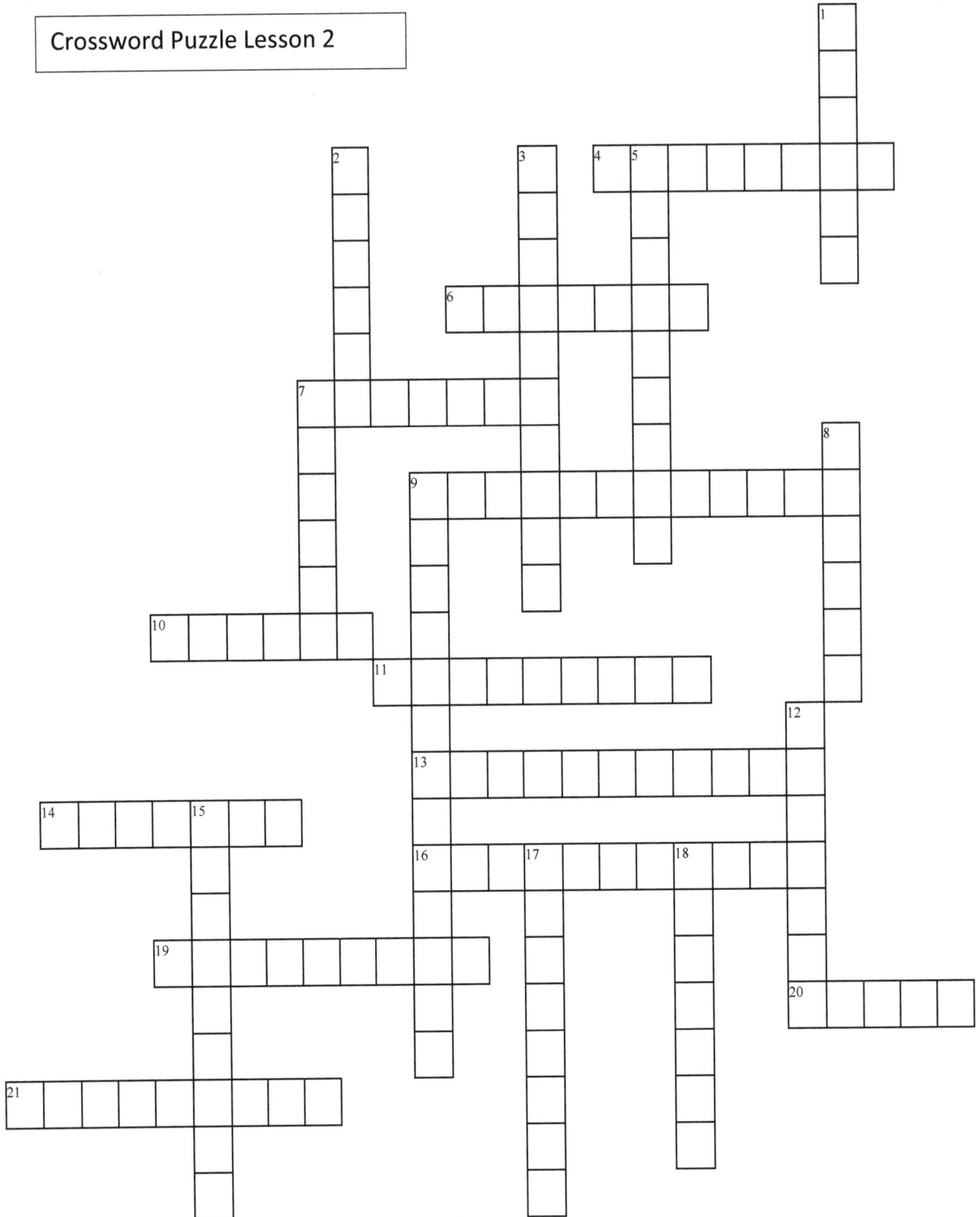

Lesson 2: Prefixes: de-, en-, em-, in-, re-, un-

Across

4. call to mind; have in or be able to bring to one's mind an awareness of (someone or something that one has seen, known, or experienced in the past)

6. a natural instinctive state of mind deriving from one's circumstances, mood, or relationships with others

7. to aid in the growth of

9. unlikely to be true

10. not seen or observed

11. unable to do or achieve (something)

13. to try to find out the facts about (something, such as a science project) in order to learn how it happened, why it happened, etc.

14. to write again

16. not requiring or relying on something else

19. cause (something) to occur in a particular way

20. take delight or pleasure in (an activity or occasion)

21. cause (someone) to feel awkward, self-conscious, or ashamed

Down

1. place trust

2. lacking the skill, means, or opportunity to do something

3. not finished

5. faced with something difficult or hostile

7. come to a resolution in the mind as a result of consideration

8. to fix or mend a thing suffering from damage

9. not limited

12. make new

15. to explain or tell the meaning of

17. a flat paper container with a sealable flap, used to enclose a letter or document

18. put an end to the existence of (something) by damaging or attacking it

Word Bank				
decide	envelope	incomplete	repair	unable
depend	encounter	incapable	restore	unbelievable
destroy	enjoy	independent	repaint	unconditional
determine	emotional	investigate	remember	unseen
develop	embarrass	interpret		

Review Lesson 2: Prefixes: de-, en-, em-, in-, re-, un-

Now that you have finished lesson 1 which helped you understand the meaning of the following prefixes:

de-

en- or em-

in-

re-

un-

You should see your reading comprehension, writing and communications skills improve.

Answer the following questions: (There are no right or wrong answers.)

1) Did you find this lesson helpful? Why or why not?

_____

_____

2) What 3 things are you going to do differently as a result of this lesson when you read a book or text or have an assignment?

_____

_____

3) Do you think knowing these prefixes will improve your communication skills?

_____

_____

4) Do you think knowing these prefixes will improve your reading comprehension?

_____

_____

LESSON 3

Page Left Blank Intentionally

As discussed in the student letter, you will learn the meaning of the following prefixes through 5 activities:

Word Bank of Prefixes		
ad- to, toward	co-, con-, com- against	mis- wrong; bad
pre- before, less than	pro- not; opposite	

As you complete each activity, I want you think about how you can use the knowledge of knowing prefixes to improve your reading comprehension, your writing and your communication skills.

I recommend that you use http://www.dictionary.com, oxforddictionaries.com and an actual dictionary to complete the activities. Let's get started!..

Lesson 3: Prefixes: ad-, com-, con-, mis-, pre-, pro-

Word Bank of Prefixes		
ad- to, toward	co-, con-, com- against	mis- wrong; bad
pre- before, less than	pro- not; opposite	

Word Study or Analysis: Do a word study or analysis of the above prefixes by using of the words below, each word contains one of the prefixes. REMEMBER to look for patterns in the definitions of words with the same prefix.

	Word	Definition	Synonym	Antonym
1.	adapt			
2.	addition			
3.	adjust			
4.	admire			
5.	advance			
6.	combine			
7.	community			
8.	compare			
9.	context			
10.	contrast			
11.	miscellaneous			
12.	miserable			
13.	mistake			
14.	misinterpret			
15.	mistake			
16.	predict			
17.	precede			
18.	precise			
19.	prevent			
20.	proactive			
21.	proceed			
22.	provide			
23.	prompt			

Lesson 3: Prefixes: ad-, com-, con-, mis-, pre-, pro-

Word Bank of Prefixes		
ad- to, toward	co-, con-, com- against	mis- wrong; bad
pre- below, less than	pro- for; favor	

Word Bank				
adapt	combine	miscellaneous	predict	proactive
addition	community	miserable	precede	proceed
adjust	compare	mistake	precise	provide
admire	context	misinterpret	prevent	prompt
advance	contrast	mistake		

Read the sentence, then use the words in the sentence to determine the meaning (context clues) of the word that is missing. Fill in the blank.

1. In science, we use the evidence we collected to _____ the outcome of the experiment.

2. In a list, the number one will always _____ number two.

3. Math problems must have a _____ answer.

4. A traffic light is needed at the intersection to _____ car accidents.

5. The crossing guard told us when to _____ to cross the street.

6. The field trip form stated we had to _____ our own lunch.

7. The stomach virus made him feel _____.

8. I made a _____ by not studying for the test.

9. If you _____ the question, you will answer it incorrectly.

10. If you want to make good grades, you must be _____ by studying.

11. It is important to be _____ when you have an appointment.

12. Some animals _____ their physical appearance to blend into their environment.

13. My classmates bought _____ items to the party.

14. You solve an _____ problem by finding the sum of numbers.

Lesson 3: Prefixes: ad-, com-, con-, mis-, pre-, pro-

Word Bank of Prefixes		
ad- to, toward	co-, con-, com- against	mis- wrong; bad
pre- before, less than	pro- for; favor	

Word Bank				
adapt	combine	miscellaneous	predict	proactive
addition	community	miserable	precede	proceed
adjust	compare	mistake	precise	provide
admire	context	misinterpret	prevent	prompt
advance	contrast	mistake		

(continued from previous page)

15. The team had to _____ themselves on the bench to make room for one more person.

16. We went the beach so that we could _____ the sunset.

17. I want to make sure that I _____ to the next grade level so I must make time to study.

18. I had to write an essay to compare and _____ baseball and basketball.

19. He lives in a town with a _____ swimming pool.

20. In biology lab we do independent experiments, then we _____ the results with our lab partner's.

21. After reading the story, I understood the _____ of the questions about it.

22. The taste of the lemon can't _____ with that of an orange; an orange tastes much better.

23. It is easy to _____ the meaning of words if you don't understand the context of them.

Lesson 3: Prefixes: ad-, com-, con-, mis-, pre-, pro-

Word Bank of Prefixes		
ad-	com-, con-	mis-
pre-	pro-	

Question: What pattern do I see in the meaning of the words with the same prefix? Answer in complete sentences.

1. What is the pattern I see in the meaning of the words that begin with the prefix ad-?

_____

_____

2. What is the pattern I see in the meaning of the words that begin with the prefix com- and con-?

_____

_____

3. What is the pattern I see in the meaning of the words that begin with the prefix mis-?

_____

_____

4. What is the pattern I see in the meaning of the words that begin with the prefix pre-?

_____

_____

5. What is the pattern I see in the meaning of the words that begin with the prefix pro-?

_____

_____

Lesson 3: Prefixes: ad-, com-, con-, mis-, pre-, pro-

Now, it's your turn. **Do-It Yourself** (DIY) word study. Think of words you know which begin with the prefixes learned in this lesson. Do a word study on the words you think of.

1. Do you know any words that begin with ad-? List 2. (If you don't know any, look in the dictionary.)

_____

2. Do a word study on your 2 words.

Word	Definition	Synonym	Antonym

3. Do you know any words that begin with com- and con-? List 2. (If you don't know any, look in the dictionary.)

_____

4. Do a word study on your 2 words.

Word	Definition	Synonym	Antonym

5. Do you know any words that begin with mis-? List 2. (If you don't know any, look in the dictionary.)

_____

6. Do a word study on your 2 words.

Word	Definition	Synonym	Antonym

Lesson 3: Prefixes: ad-, com-, con-, mis-, pre-, pro-

It's your turn. Think of words you know which begin with the prefixes. Do a word study on the words you think of. (continued from previous page)

7. Do you know any words that begin with pro-? List 2. (If you don't know any, look in the dictionary.)

_____

8. Do a word study on your 2 words.

Word	Definition	Synonym	Antonym

Lesson 3: Prefixes: ad-, com-, con-, mis-, pre-, pro-

Crossword Puzzle

Crossword Puzzle Lesson 3

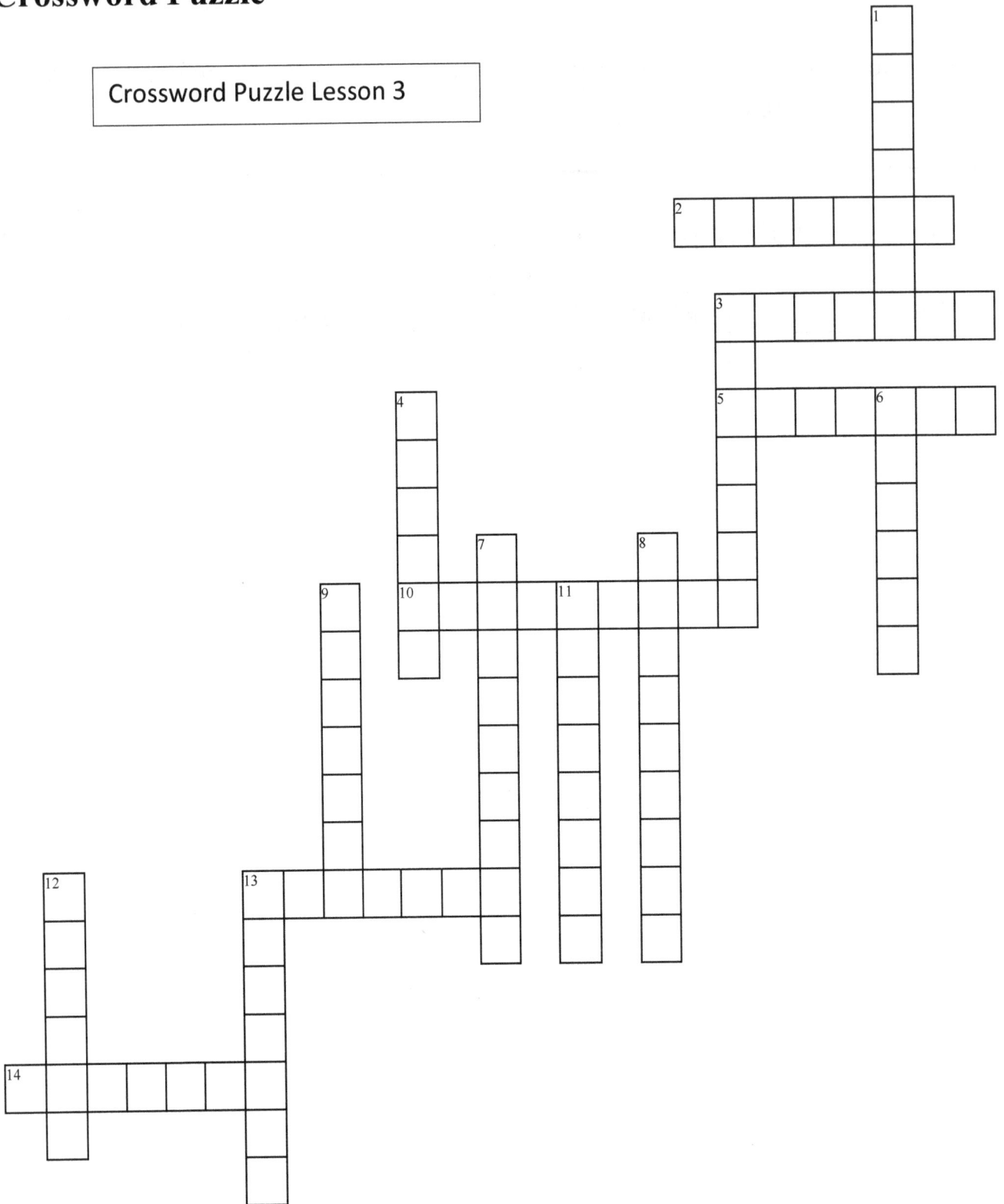

Lesson 3: Prefixes: ad-, com-, con-, mis-, pre-, pro-

Across

2. to stop something from happening

3. whole situation, background, or environment relevant to a particular event, personality, creation, etc.

5. an act or judgement that is misguided or wrong

10. creating or controlling a situation by causing something to happen rather than responding to it after it has happened

13. to say what one believes will happen before it happens

14. to supply or make available

Down

1. move forward, typically in a purposeful way

3. to examine in order to observe or discover similarities or differences

4. done, spoken, etc. at once or without delay

6. to change so as to fit, conform, make suitable, etc.

7. a group of people living in the same place or having a particular characteristic in common

8. unhappy; uncomfortable

9. to come or bring into union; act or mix together; unite; join

11. to show differences between two or more subjects, objects, places, etc.

12. to regard with wonder, delight, and pleased approval

13. to go before

Word Bank*				
adapt	combine	miscellaneous	predict	proactive
addition	community	miserable	precede	proceed
adjust	compare	mistake	precise	provide
admire	context	misinterpret	prevent	prompt
advance	contrast	mistake		

***Note:** All of the words from the word bank will not be used.

Review Lesson 3: Prefixes: ad-, com-, con-, mis-, pre-, pro-

Now that you have finished lesson 1 which helped you understand the meaning of the following prefixes:

ad-

com- or con-

mis-

pre-

pro-

You should see your reading comprehension, writing and communications skills improve.

Answer the following questions: (There are no right or wrong answers.)

1) Did you find this lesson helpful? Why or why not?

_____

_____

2) What 3 things are you going to do differently as a result of this lesson when you read a book or text or have an assignment?

_____

_____

3) Do you think knowing these prefixes will improve your communication skills?

_____

_____

4) Do you think knowing these prefixes will improve your reading comprehension?

_____

_____

4 ANSWERS

Page Left Blank Intentionally

Word	Definition	Synonym	Antonym
antivirus	a type of software designed to prevent viruses from breaking the computer	not applicable (n/a)	not applicable (n/a)
antisocial	avoiding the company of other people	unsociable	affable, gregarious
antidote	a medicine or other remedy for counteracting the effects of poison, disease, etc.		cure
antifreeze	a liquid used in the radiator of an internal-combustion engine to lower the freezing point of the cooling medium	not applicable (n/a)	not applicable (n/a)
antibody	any of numerous Y -shaped protein molecules produced by B cells as a primary immune defense, each molecule and its clones having a unique binding site that can combine with the complementary site of a foreign antigen, as on a virus or bacterium, thereby disabling the antigen and signaling other immune defenses		
ex-student	former student	not applicable (n/a)	student
ex-president	former president	not applicable (n/a)	president
ex-member	former member	non-member	member
explain	to make plain or clear	interpret, justify	confuse
exist	to be living	survive, remain	cease
disappear	to cease to be visible	vanish	visible
disagree	to argue	contradict	agree
dislike	to have hatred toward something	abhor	like, admire
disconnect	to take apart	detach, sever	connect
disgrace	the loss of respect, honor, or esteem	dishonor, disapprove	honor
nonsense	craziness, ridiculousness	foolishness	sense
nonstop	continuous, direct	express, endless	stopping
nonviolent	peaceful	passive	violent
nonfiction	story based on real facts and information	not applicable (n/a)	fiction
underweight	deficiency in weight below a standard or requirement	malnourished	overweight
understudy	substitute for another actor	backup	not applicable (n/a)
underwater	underneath the water's surface	submerged	not applicable (n/a)
underground	beneath the surface of the ground	buried	aboveground

1. under
2. anti
3. non
4. dis
5. ex-
6. anti
7. ex-
8. under
9. dis
10. non
11. anti
12. dis
13. dis
14. ex
15. non
16. ex
17. under
18. dis
19. ex-
20. non
21. anti
22. anti
23. under

Page 9

1. Answer will vary, but the wording should be similar; All the words with anti- as a prefix mean against something.
2. Answer will vary, but the wording should be similar; All the words with dis- as a prefix mean not or opposite something.
3. Answer will vary, but the wording should be similar; All the words with ex- as a prefix mean out of or from something.
4. Answer will vary, but the wording should be similar; All the words with non- as a prefix mean not something.
5. Answer will vary, but the wording should be similar; All the words with under- as a prefix mean less than or below something.

Page 10 and 11 DIY (Do it yourself) Word Study

The assignment is two pages long. The answers will vary because the child or student must think of their own words that use the prefixes learned in the lesson. How to check it? Simply review the words he or she wrote, ensure he or she used a dictionary and didn't use words already found in the lesson. If they can't think of any word, he or she should look in the dictionary for a word to use.

Page 12 and 13

Crossword Puzzle Lesson 1

Across

3. dislike

4. nonsense

7. ex-student

8. antidote

10. nonfiction

11. explain

13. underground

14. ex-member

16. underwater

20. disconnect

22. disagree

Down

1. nonstop

2. disgrace

4. nonviolent

5. ex-president

6. disappear

9. understudy

12. underweight

15. antisocial

17. antifreeze

18. antivirus

19. antibody

21. exist

Word	Definition	Synonym	Antonym
decide	come to a resolution in the mind as a result of consideration	settle	unsettle
depend	place trust	rely on	distrust
destroy	put an end to the existence of (something) by damaging or attacking it	demolish	build
determine	to fix exactly or with authority	decide	overlook
develop	to aid in the growth of	grow	decrease
envelope	a flat paper container with a sealable flap, used to enclose a letter or document	wrapper	not applicable (n/a)
encounter	faced with something difficult or hostile	experience	retreat
enjoy	take delight or pleasure in (an activity or occasion)	like	dislike
emotion	a natural instinctive state of mind deriving from one's circumstances, mood, or relationships with others	feeling	unemotional
embarrass	cause (someone) to feel awkward, self-conscious, or ashamed	shame	cheer
incomplete	not finished	unfinished	complete
incapable	unable to do or achieve (something)	unskillful	skillful
independent	not requiring or relying on something else	self-sufficient	helpless
investigate	to try to find out the facts about (something, such as a science project) in order to learn how it happened, why it happened, etc.	explore	
interpret	to explain or tell the meaning of	explain	confuse
repair	to fix or mend a thing suffering from damage	fix	break
restore	make new	renew	damage
rewrite	to write again	edit	
remember	call to mind; have in or be able to bring to one's mind an awareness of (someone or something that one has seen, known, or experienced in the past)	recall	forget
unable	lacking the skill, means, or opportunity to do something	weak	able
unbelievable	unlikely to be true	incredible	believable
unconditional	not limited	unlimited	conditional
unseen	not seen or observed	invisible	seen

1. decide

2. depend

3. destroy

4. interpret

5. develop

6. envelope

7. encounter

8. enjoy

9. emotional

10. embarrass

11. incomplete

12. incapable

13. independent

14. investigate

15. determine

16. repair

17. restore

18. repaint

19. remember

20. unable

21. unbelievable

22. unconditional

23. unseen

Page 19 Lesson 2: What do the words have in common?

1. Answer will vary, but the wording should be similar; All the words with de- as a prefix mean remove from or opposite of something.
2. Answer will vary, but the wording should be similar; All the words with em- and en- as a prefix means cause to something.
3. Answer will vary, but the wording should be similar; All the words with in- as a prefix means not something. Just like un-.
4. Answer will vary, but the wording should be similar; All the words with re- as a prefix means again or back of something.
5. Answer will vary, but the wording should be similar; All the words with un- as a prefix means not something. Just like in-.

Page 20 and 21 Lesson 2 : Do it yourself (DIY word study)

The assignment is two pages long. The answers will vary because the child or student must think of their own words that use the prefixes learned in the lesson. How to check it? Simply review the words he or she wrote, ensure he or she used a dictionary and didn't use words already found in the lesson. If they can't think of any word, he or she should look in the dictionary for a word to use.

Page 22 and 23 Lesson 2: Crossword Puzzle

Across

4. remember
6. emotion
7. to aid in the growth of
9. unbelievable
10. unseen
17. incapable
13. investigate
14. rewrite
16. independent
19. determine
20. enjoy
21. embarrass

Down

1. depend
2. unable
3. incomplete
5. encounter
7. decide
8. repair
9. unconditional
12. restore
15. interpret
17. envelope
18. destroy

Word	Definition	Synonym	Antonym
adapt	to make fit or suitable by changing or adjusting	fit	incapable
addition	a joining of a thing to another thing	increase	subtraction
adjust	to change so as to fit, conform, make suitable, etc.	adapt	unorganized
admire	to regard with wonder, delight, and pleased approval	appreciate	blame
advance	move forward, typically in a purposeful way	first	last
combine	to come or bring into union; act or mix together; unite; join	connect	disconnect
community	a group of people living in the same place or having a particular characteristic in common	neighborhood	
compare	to examine in order to observe or discover similarities or differences	match	unmatched
context	whole situation, background, or environment relevant to a particular event, personality, creation, etc.	condition	
contrast	to show differences between two or more subjects, objects, places, etc.	difference	compare
miscellaneous	varied	assorted	same
miserable	unhappy; uncomfortable	discomfort	happy
mistake	an act or judgement that is misguided or wrong	error	correct
misinterpret	understand or explain incorrectly	incorrect	interpret
misunderstand	fail to interpret or understand (something) correctly	incorrect	understand
predict	to say what one believes will happen before it happens	foretell	ignore
precede	to go before	anticipate	follow
precise	to cut off, exact	actual	vague
prevent	to stop something from happening	avoid	allow
proactive	creating or controlling a situation by causing something to happen rather than responding to it after it has happened	aggressive	reactive
proceed	to go forward	continue	stop
provide	to supply or make available	bring	subtract
prompt	done, spoken, etc. at once or without delay	quick	late

Page 27 and 28 Lesson 3 Fill in the blank

1. predict
2. precede
3. precise
4. prevent
5. proceed
6. provide
7. miserable
8. mistake
9. misunderstand
10. proactive
11. prompt
12. adapt
13. miscellaneous
14. addition
15. adjust
16. admire
17. advance
18. contrast
19. community
20. combine
21. context
22. compare
23. misinterpret

Page 29 Lesson 3 What do the words have in common?

1. Answer will vary, but the wording should be similar; All the words with ad- as a prefix means to or toward something.
2. Answer will vary, but the wording should be similar; All the words with com- and con- as a prefix means against something.
3. Answer will vary, but the wording should be similar; All the words with mis- as a prefix means wrong or bad.
4. Answer will vary, but the wording should be similar; All the words with pre- as a prefix means below or less than something.
5. Answer will vary, but the wording should be similar; All the words with pro- as a prefix means for or favor.

Across

2. prevent

3. context

5. mistake

10. proactive

13. predict

14. provide

Down

1. advance

3. compare

4. prompt

6. adjust

7. community

8. miserable

9. combine

11. contrast

12. admire

13. precede

Works Cited

"Dictionary Definitions You Can Understand - YourDictionary." *Dictionary Definitions You Can*

Understand - YourDictionary. LoveToKnow Corporation, n.d. Web. 20 Jan. 2014.

<http://www.yourdictionary.com/>.

Dictionary.com. Dictionary.com, n.d. Web. 20 Jan. 2014. <http://dictionary.reference.com/>.

"Longman English Dictionary Online - LDOCE." *Longman English Dictionary Online*. Pearson ELT,

n.d. Web. 21 Dec. 2013. <http://www.ldoceonline.com/>.

White, Thomas G., Joanne Sowell, and Alice Yanagihara. "Teaching Elementary Students to Use Word-
part Clues." *JSTOR*. N.p., n.d. Web. 02 Feb. 2014.
<http://www.jstor.org/discover/10.2307/20200115?uid=3739864&uid=2134&uid=2478416493&uid=2
&uid=70&uid=3&uid=3739256&uid=60&uid=2478416483&sid=21103376109967>.

ABOUT THE AUTHOR

Julie Jones graduated from the New Jersey Institute of Technology with a BS in Business Administration with a concentration in Manager of Information Systems in 2012. She is a Certified Associate Project Manager. After a bad learning experience, she researched her learning style. She wrote this book to share that experience. She enjoys giving seminars or workshops regarding her learning experience. She lives in New Jersey with her family.